Contents

Theme park forces

Whenever I go on a ride, I'm always thinking of what's wrong with the thing and how it can be improved.

Walt Disney

Have you been to a theme park and been on an exciting ride like a roller-coaster? If you have, you would have experienced the powerful **forces** that are at work. Theme park rides push and pull. They roll and spin. They scare us and they thrill us by using the powerful forces of nature!

When we study the way theme park rides move, we are using a branch of science called physics. Physics is the study of **matter**, energy, forces and the ways things move.

Theme parks are great places to see physics in action. We see bright, flashing lights that work due to the power of electricity. We can see rides that move due to the force of gravity. In fact, there are many more forces at work in a theme park that help to make them so much fun! Come on, let's take a look!

Did you know?
The Scenic Railway was built in Melbourne's Luna Park in 1912. It is the world's oldest continually operating roller-coaster. It is unusual because it needs to be slowed down by a person who sits in the middle and operates a brake.

forces invisible pushes or pulls that act on objects to make them move
matter objects and things that take up space

Roller-coasters can be scary, but they are a lot of fun!

LET'S FIND OUT

- Why are theme park rides so much fun?
- What forces are used in theme park rides?
- How do roller-coasters move?
- What can experiments teach us about forces in rides with loops?
- How do you ride a Toaster Coaster?

How a roller-coaster moves

Riding on a roller-coaster is a lot of fun. It's also a great way to learn about the forces that affect our lives every day.

Roller-coasters travel at very high speeds. They are able to turn corners, through dips and peaks, and even do 360-degree loops! You might think roller-coasters are powered by engines. But, most of them aren't powered by anything that is **human-made**. They travel using bursts of energy to keep them moving until the ride stops. So, where do they get this energy? The simple answer is: they use the force of **gravity**.

A roller-coaster ride begins with a push or a pull to the highest point on the track. Some roller-coasters are pulled up by a motor-powered chain. Others are pushed up by a system called a launch.

The launch pushes the roller-coaster upwards using air, magnets or liquid.

1. The roller-coaster is pushed or pulled to the highest point.

2. Then, gravity pulls the roller-coaster downwards.

human-made made by humans, not made by nature
gravity the force of attraction between two objects

When the roller-coaster reaches its highest point, off it goes! The force of gravity takes over and pulls the roller-coaster downwards. Gravity gives the roller-coaster the energy it needs to continue until the end of the ride. The energy supplied by gravity helps the roller-coaster stay on the tracks. It also keeps the riders safely in their seats.

Most roller-coasters have three sets of wheels that grip the track. One set sits on top of the track and one sits beneath it. The third set grips the sides of the track. It stops the roller-coaster from moving sideways.

After a few minutes, the roller-coaster reaches the end of the track and stops. It has used up most of the energy the force of gravity has given to it.

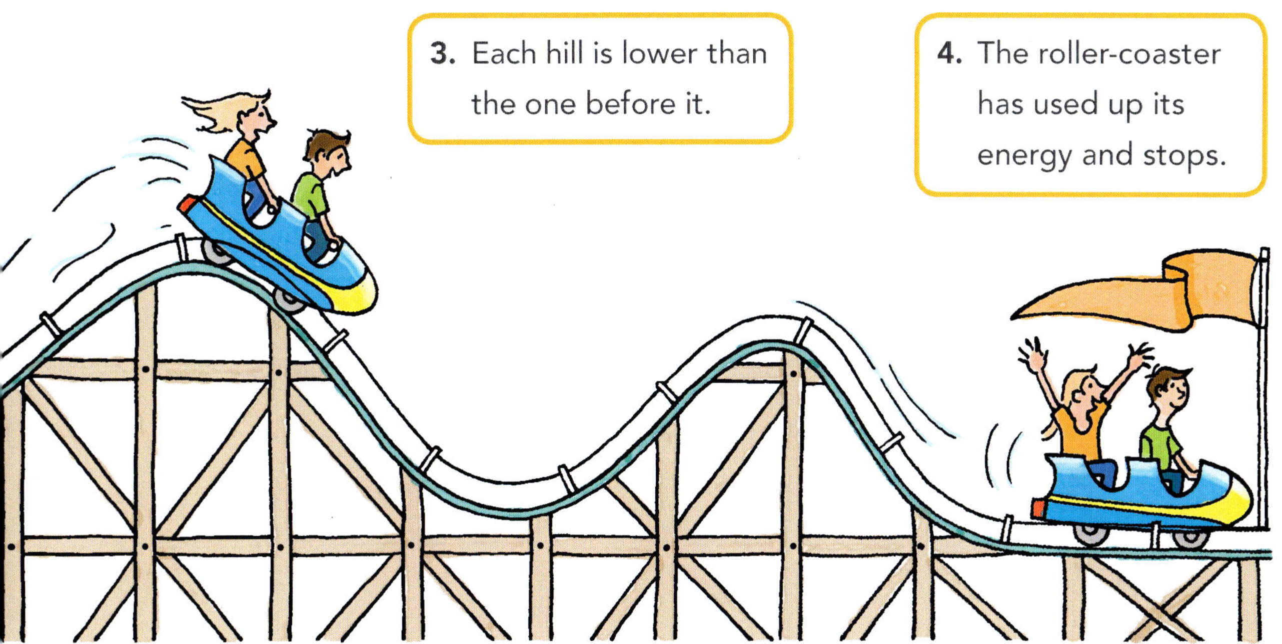

Breakaway tasks

Remembering

1 What is the main force that gives a roller-coaster energy?

2 How many sets of wheels do most roller-coasters have?

Understanding

3 Draw a picture of what might happen at the start of a ride if the roller-coaster cannot climb high enough.

Applying

4 Make a timeline to show the stages in a roller-coaster's journey. Begin with the passengers climbing on. Finish with the roller-coaster coming to a stop at the end of the ride.

5 Write a short report about a roller-coaster you have been on, or have seen on TV.

Analysing

6 Make a list of safety features you would check for if you were responsible for running a roller-coaster.

7 Research and write a report about a famous roller-coaster in another country.

Evaluating

8 What is your favourite type of roller-coaster? Write a list of the features you like most about it.

9 Look online to find footage of a roller-coaster. Make a list of changes you would make to it to make it even more fun.

Creating

10 Design and draw your own roller-coaster car. You could model it on an animal, or a fast-moving vehicle. Be as creative as you like, but make it safe to ride.

Make a roller-loop

Many theme park rides, including roller-coasters, travel in loops that turn the riders upside down. In these rides, we experience a force that pushes us outwards. It feels like the ride is stopping us from falling or flying away.

Here's an experiment that uses a **similar** force.

Materials

- a paper cup
- a pen or a pencil
- string
- a coin
- water – about 1 cup

Method

1. First, use the pen or pencil to make a hole in one side of the cup, just below the top. Then, make another hole in the same place on the other side of the cup.

2. Cut a piece of the string. It needs to be about 120 centimetres long.

3. Tie each end of the string through one of the holes in the cup. This forms a handle. Your roller-loop is now ready!

similar nearly the same

4. Take your roller-loop outside. Make sure you are a safe distance from other people or anything you could hit. Place the coin in the cup.

5. Using the string handle, swing the cup in circles above your head. The coin should stay in the cup as it spins around. Keep the cup spinning fast so that the coin doesn't fall out.

6. Next, lower your hand to the side of your body. Keep the cup swinging until it is spinning in a sideways circle like a roller-coaster loop.

7. Repeat the experiment using water instead of the coin. Again, the water should remain in the cup as you swing it around!

Results

Congratulations! You have just made and operated your own roller-loop! Your arm supplied the force that kept the coin and the water from falling out of the cup.

Breakaway tasks

Remembering

1 How many items do you need to do this experiment?

2 What substance are you asked to put in the cup after you've tried the experiment using a coin?

Understanding

3 Write a paragraph about a time you have felt a similar kind of force, for example in a vehicle or a similar theme park ride.

4 Draw a diagram to show what will happen to the water or coin if the cup isn't swung quickly enough.

Applying

5 Perform the experiment again, holding the string handle only halfway along. How does this affect the speed at which it needs to spin in a circle?

Analysing

6 Write a short report about your experiment. Include an introduction, list of materials, the method and the results.

7 Write safety guidelines for other students who will perform this experiment.

Evaluating

8 Do you think the instructions for the experiment were detailed enough? Why/why not?

9 Research some other looping rides you could try. Draw a diagram of the three you'd like to try the most.

Creating

10 Design your own exciting looping ride. Consider using an animal, such as a snake, as the basis for your design. Present it as a poster.

Force Kitchen Max!

+ www.forcekitchenmax.com.au

Home | Rides | Visitor information

It's finally here, the theme park that will make your tummy rumble in more ways than one – ***Force Kitchen Max!***

Force Kitchen Max is the newest, tastiest theme park in Australia. Our exciting rides will leave you breathless and hungry for more!

Force Kitchen Max is home to the most special and fastest rides – EVER!

Force Kitchen Max is not only the place to be seen; it's the place to be green! All of our rides and attractions are powered by **sustainable** sources. The sun rolls our coasters. The wind spins our wheels.

We've even built the world's first solar-powered open-air dodgem rink – the Kitchen Sink Rink! No more sparks, no more wires – at Force Kitchen Max, dodgems are the planet's best friend!
So don't waste your time and money elsewhere. Click here to book your tasty tickets online now.

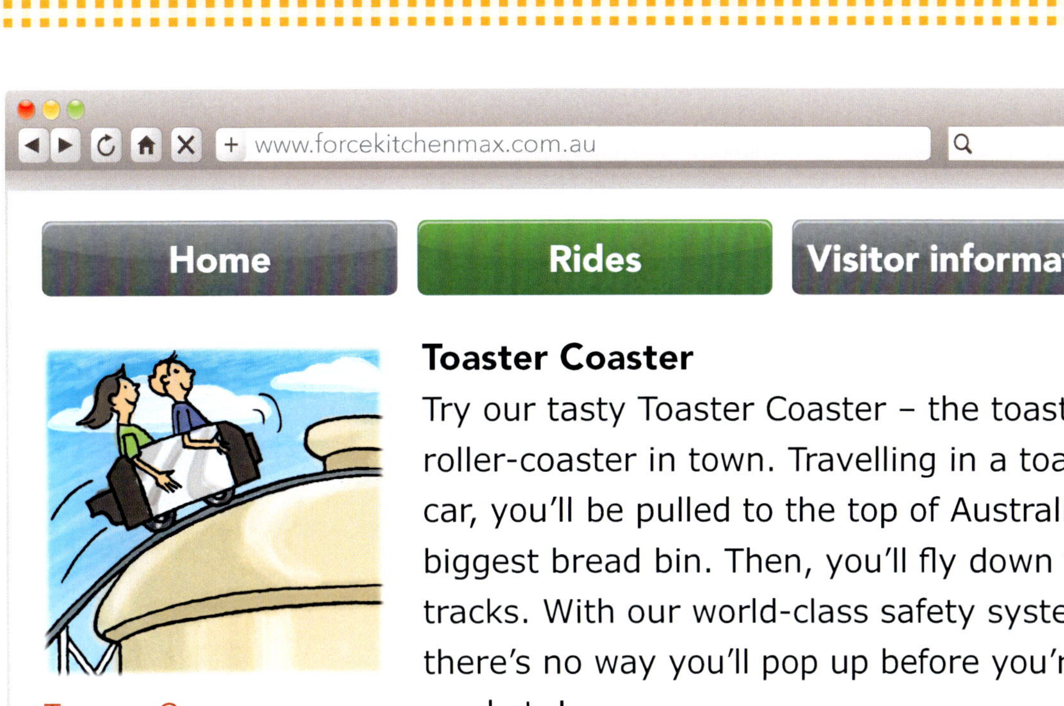

Toaster Coaster

Toaster Coaster

Try our tasty Toaster Coaster – the toastiest roller-coaster in town. Travelling in a toaster car, you'll be pulled to the top of Australia's biggest bread bin. Then, you'll fly down the tracks. With our world-class safety system, there's no way you'll pop up before you're ready to!

Scooper-Looper

Scooper-Looper

Grab a seat on our Scooper-Looper – the world's fastest looping ice-cream scoop. The force of four spinning scoops will leave you a bit dizzy but you'll be dribbling with delight!

Pop and Drop

Pop and Drop

Feel the force of gravity on the amazing Pop and Drop pole ride. You'll be popped out of a giant toaster, to a height of 90 metres. Then, you'll be pushed back down with the full force of gravity. You'll have a soft landing back in the toaster. But look out – your stomach might stay up in the sky!

sustainable something that won't do long-term damage to the environment

Breakaway tasks

Remembering

1 What is the name of the roller-coaster?
2 How are the rides powered?

Understanding

3 Find an example of sustainable power in the text. Draw a diagram showing how you think it might work.
4 Why are there 'no sparks and wires' in the dodgem car rink at Force Kitchen Max? Write a short description of how a solar-powered dodgem car might look.

Applying

5 Write a letter to a friend, convincing him or her to come to Force Kitchen Max with you.
6 List the real-life rides you know and place under the headings (Push and Pull) according to the main force felt by people on the ride.

Analysing

7 Identify the main intention of the writer. Is it to give an accurate impression of the theme park, or to achieve another purpose?
8 Find an example of a sentence that clearly shows the writer's opinion rather than the facts.

Evaluating

9 Make a table of the rides mentioned in the text. Beside each ride, write an improvement to make the ride more fun, or safer.

Creating

10 Make a cardboard model of a ride you would like to see at Force Kitchen Max. What shapes or objects will you use?

The Beast

***The Beast* is a book by American writer R. L. Stine about two children who get locked in a theme park after it has closed for the night. R. L. Stine has written hundreds of children's books, many of them scary…**

Chapter One

I shut my eyes as a shrill scream escaped my throat.

Bouncing hard, I opened them in time to see the trees fly by in a jarring blur. "Whoa!" I was tossed forward as I roared straight down into darkness.

A sudden spin made me cry out again. The car tilted hard to the left and I slammed into my cousin, Ashley Franks. She was screaming, too. Her blond hair flew out wildly behind her head.

We swooped down once more, a sharp dip. I yelped in surprise as I felt myself fly up from the seat. The trees whirred by, shadowy in the dark night light. The car clattered noisily as it began to climb again.

"This is great!" I screamed to Ashley.

Her face was bright red. Her blue eyes were wide, staring up to the top of the track. She grinned at me and started to reply. But instead, she let out a startled whoop as our car plunged down.

Down, down with a deafening roar.

The wind battered my face. I gripped the bar tightly with both hands. Down, down – and into total darkness.

"Huh?"

A tunnel. We whirred through the tunnel, then back out into the dim light filtering through the dark, leafy trees. Then a jolting turn pushed me into Ashley again. My cousin was screaming too hard to notice.

Another tunnel. Another climb. Another swooping, roaring spin that made the car squeal.

And then we slowed to a stop.

Over my thudding heartbeat I could hear screams and laughter behind us. Ashley and I had been riding in the front car.

I turned to her. She was still breathing hard. Her hair was wild, standing almost straight up. She was trying to brush it down with both hands.

"You were right, James!" she exclaimed. "The Beast®
is awesome!"

Breakaway tasks

Remembering

1 What is the name of the character telling us the story?
2 Which car of the roller-coaster did the characters ride in?

Understanding

3 In your own words, write a summary of the main points of the story.
4 Draw an illustration to show how the characters' faces might look as they zoom down into the tunnel.

Applying

5 Use your knowledge of The Beast to draw a simple diagram that shows what the roller-coaster in the story might look like.
6 Use the story's descriptions of The Beast to make a list of roller-coaster features that would guarantee a fun ride.

Analysing

7 What feelings do you think the author wants us to experience as we read this section of the story? Draw a large circle on a piece of paper and turn it into a 'smilie' icon to capture this feeling.
8 What do you think might have happened immediately before the beginning of Chapter One? Write a paragraph that could be read before the chapter begins.

Evaluating

9 Write down two features you would add to this roller-coaster to make it even scarier.

Creating

10 Imagine you are in the roller-coaster with James and Ashley. Rewrite the passage from your point of view.

Strands in action

Core tasks

1 Design your own theme park!
Start by thinking of an interesting idea for your park. Draw a map of your theme park and include labelled pictures of each ride.

2 Write an ad for TV for your theme park by making a storyboard. A storyboard is a like a comic strip. It will show how your ad will look. Each frame could highlight a particular attraction in your park. Write the words that you would like to be heard with each frame.

Extra tasks

1 Write a jingle for radio for your theme park.
Make a recording of it, and share it with the class.

2 Make a list of everyday activities in which you experience forces similar to those in theme park rides.

3 Write a limerick about a ride in the theme park you've designed. Make the ride sound as good as you can!

4 Survey your class, family and friends about their favourite types of theme park rides. Make a graph that shows how the rides compare in popularity.

When you write instructions for an experiment or a procedure, use short, clear sentences to explain each step. This way your reader will be able to follow your instructions without getting confused!

limerick a funny poem that has five lines. Lines 1, 2, and 5 rhyme with one another. Lines 3 and 4 rhyme with each other. Limericks have a distinctive rhythm.